VICTORIA

THE HIGH LIFE

SPICE GIRLS
OFFICIAL PUBLICATION

Research
Noam Friedlander

Design
JMP Ltd

Photography
The Spice Girls' families
Ray Burmiston
Rankin Waddell
Alex Bailey
Michael Ginsberg
Adrian Green

Spice Girls Management
Simon Fuller @ 19 Management

Thanks to
Catri Drummond
James Freedman
Sally Hudson
Gerrard Tyrrell

A Zone production

The author and publishers have made every reasonable effort to contact all copyright holders. Any errors that may have occurred are inadvertent and anyone who for any reason has not been contacted is invited to write to the publishers so that a full acknowledgement may be made in subsequent editions of this work.

This book is sold subject to the condition that it shall not by way of trade or otherwise be lent, resold, hired or otherwise circulated without the prior written consent of the Spice Girls in any form other than that which it has been published.

Copyright © Spice Girls Ltd 1997.
All rights reserved.
All photographs reproduced by kind permission of The Spice Girls.

The right of the Spice Girls to be identified as the authors of this book has been asserted by them in accordance with the Copyright, Designs and Patents Act 1988.

Second edition
First published in 1997 by
Zone/Chameleon Books
an imprint of Andre Deutsch Ltd.
a member of the VCI plc Group
106 Great Russell Street
London WCIB 3LJ
in association with 19 Management Ltd
Printed in Italy by G. Canale & C. Turin

CIP Data for this title is available from the British Library

ISBN 0223 99325 8

"This is your host, **Victoria**, welcoming you to my very own, official Posh Spice minibook. Thanks for choosing me – I guarantee you won't be disappointed by what I've created for you! ..."

"I don't see myself as someone who people look up to. I think the band as a whole is a role model, but not me as a person, because each of us has a different kind of fan and the younger ones don't seem to go for me."

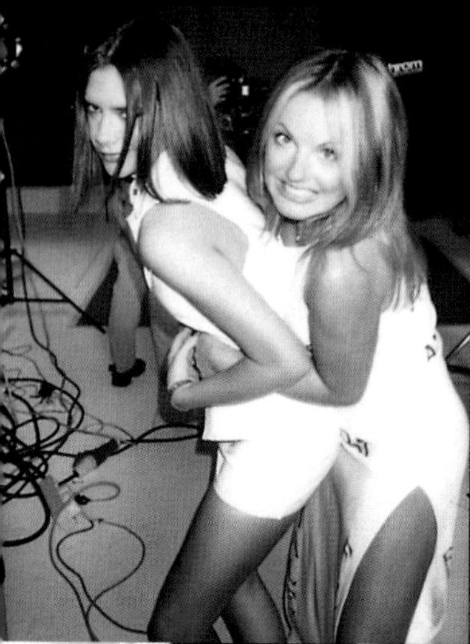
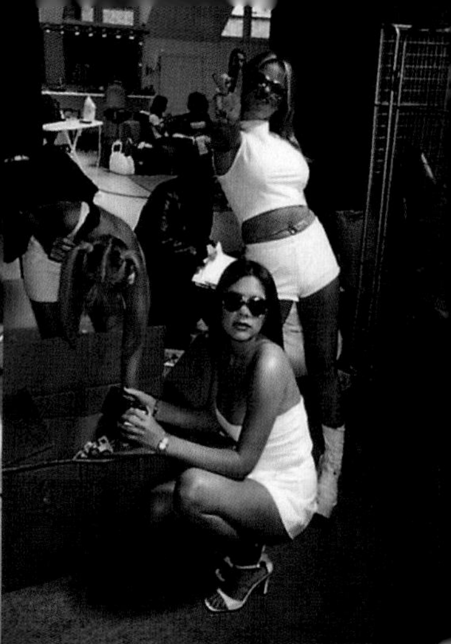
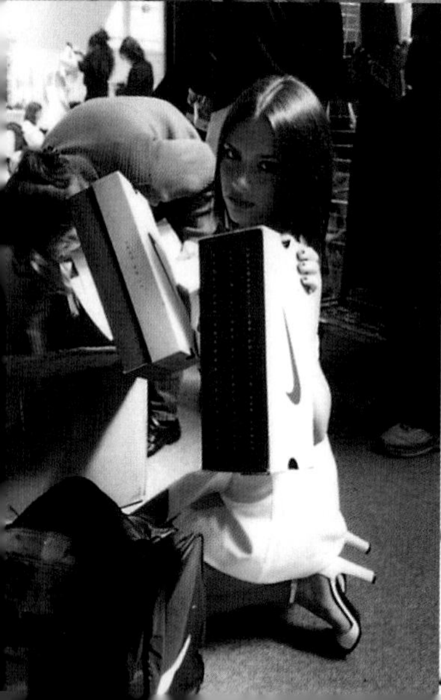
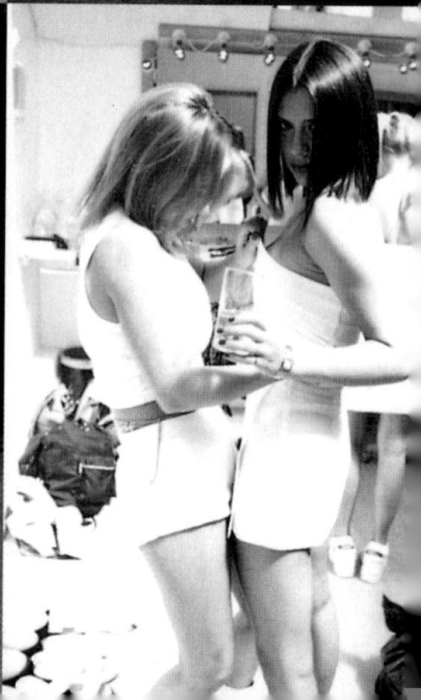

"It's probably because I've always had to work hard to prove myself that I've got to this stage."

"My favourite shops are **Prada** and **Gucci.** I don't really ever go to high street stores."

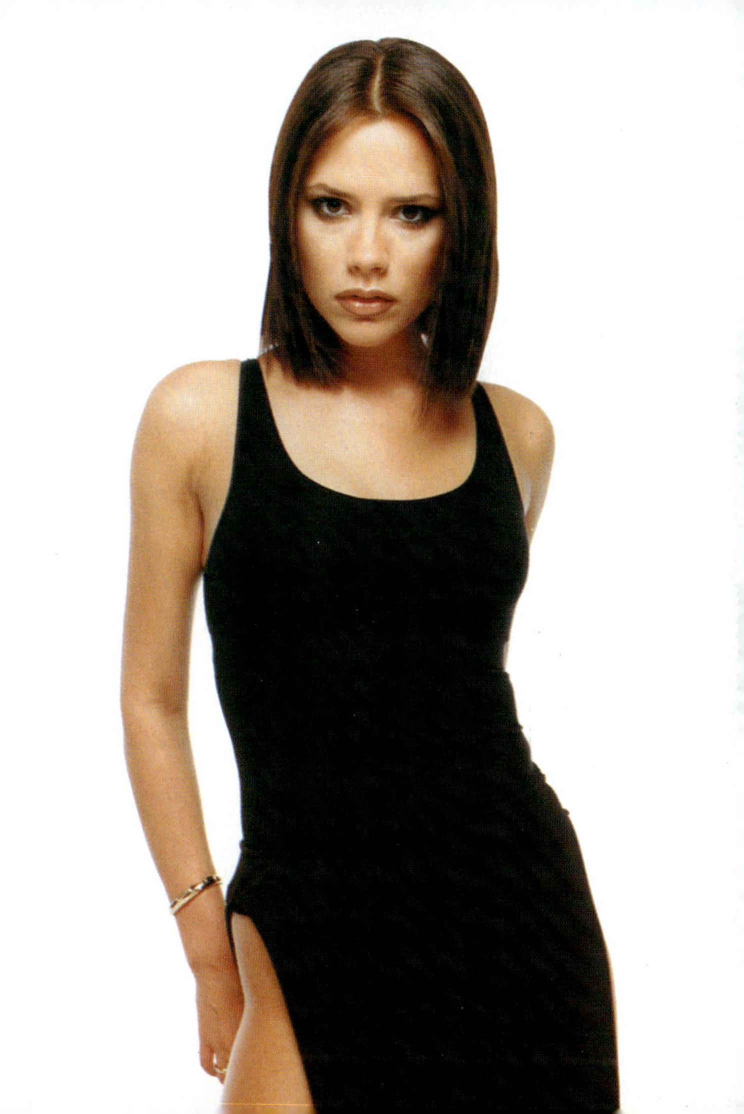

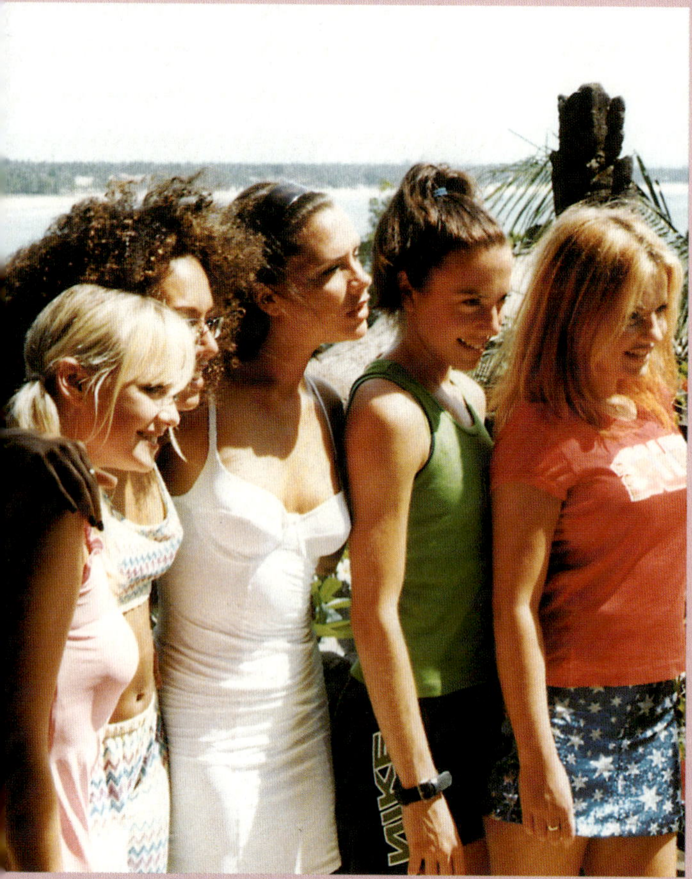

"I think it's really important to treat people the same whoever they are. Whatever their job is, however famous they are, all five of us would never treat anybody differently."

"What has changed is that we're really busy now, so we don't get to spend as much time at home and we all like being at home."

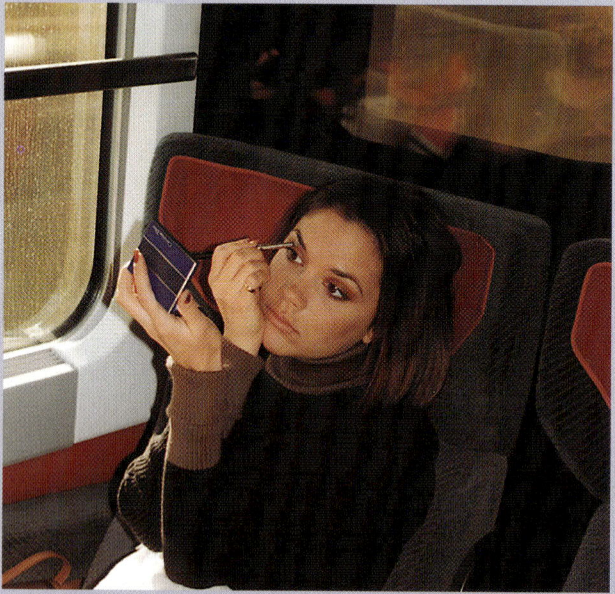

"I might be called a snob, but I like expensive make-up. If you spend a lot of money on clothes, then you might as well spend a lot on what's going on your face. I like autumny colours, like dark brown, dark orange and grey."

"I'm still me even after all that's happened. If my family told me I'd changed I'd be in big, big trouble, but they don't."

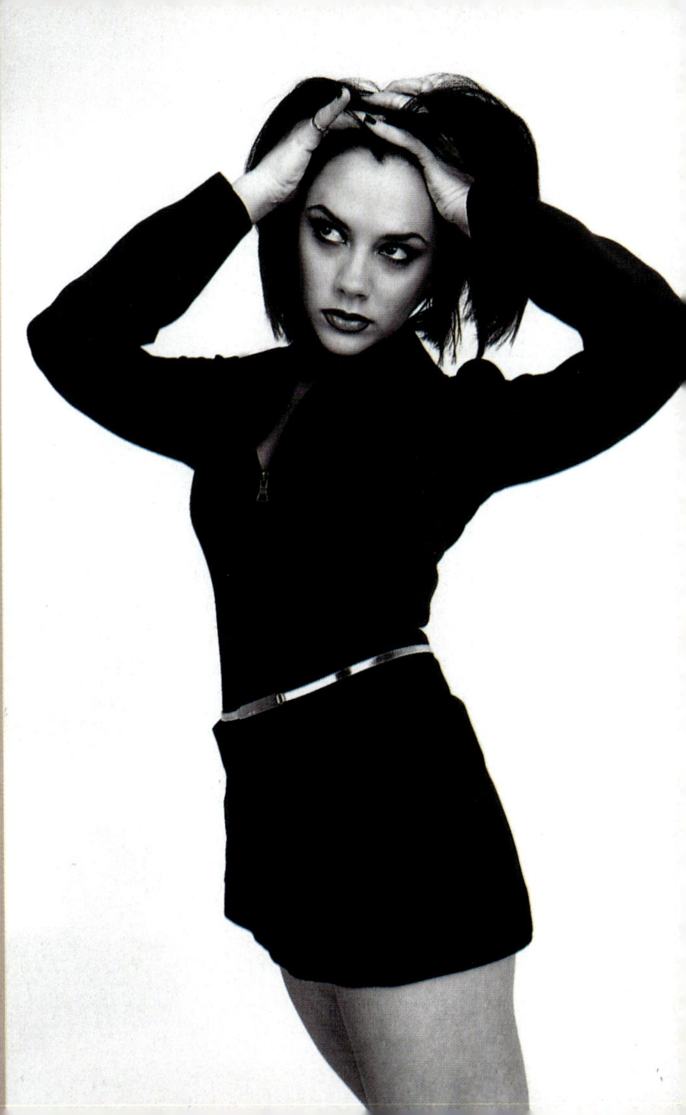

"We want to be positive role models for young girls and women."

"I wear what I wear because I want to wear it, not just because I think men might like it. In my opinion, it can be powerful when a woman wears a short skirt, a jacket and high heels – that's power dressing. (I think I must have been Joan Collins in a previous life)."

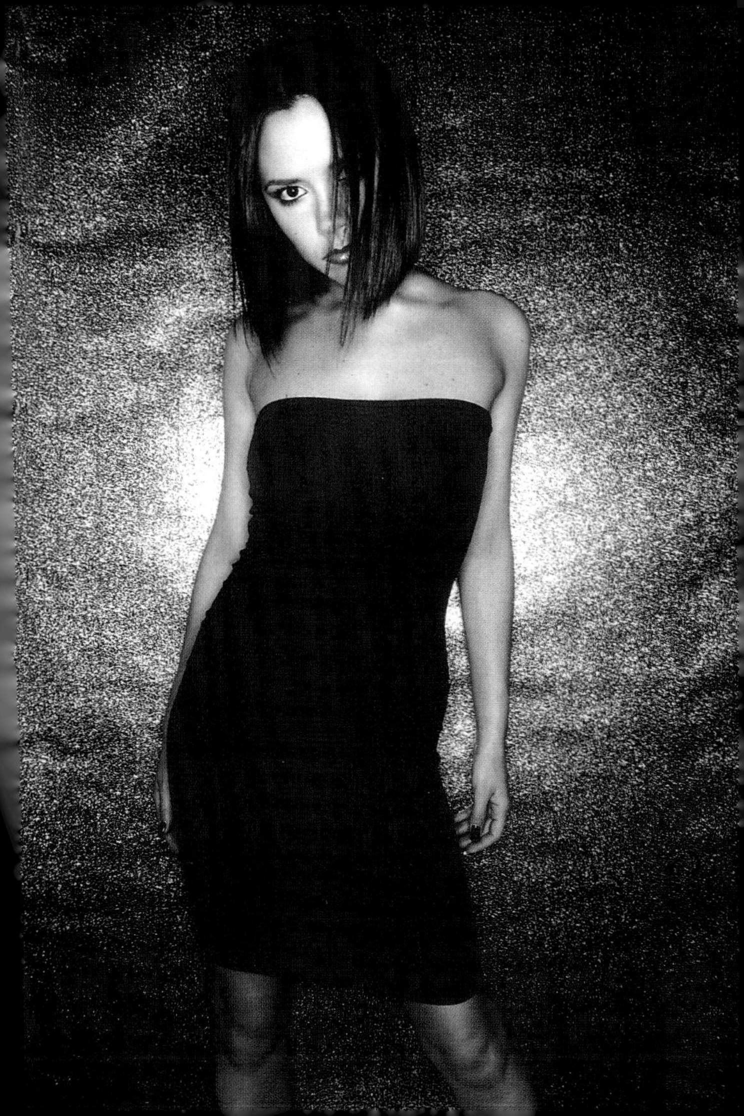

"I really enjoy travelling the world, meeting fantastic people, having fun and doing what I most enjoy – performing."

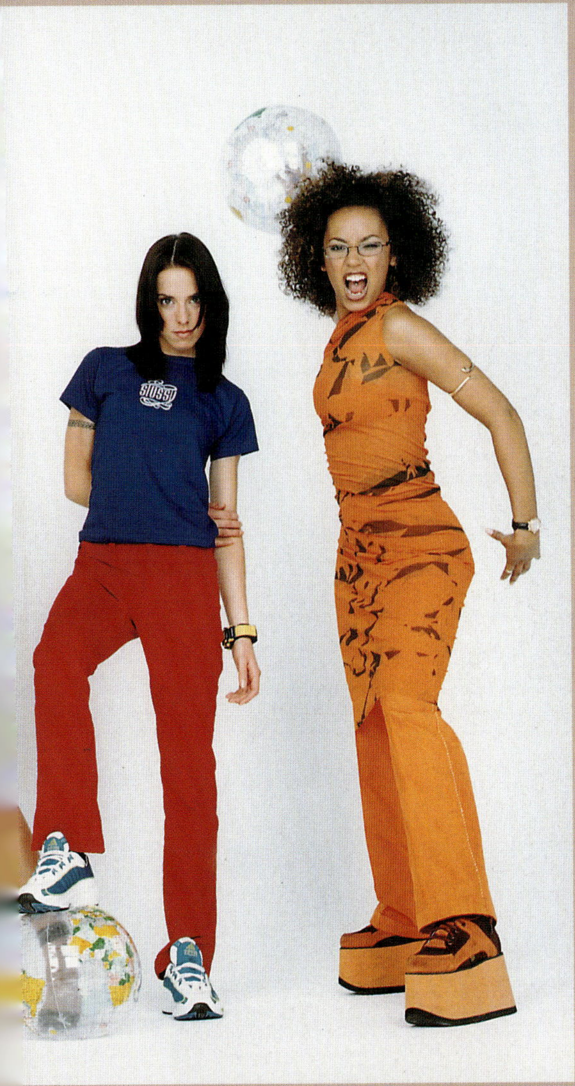

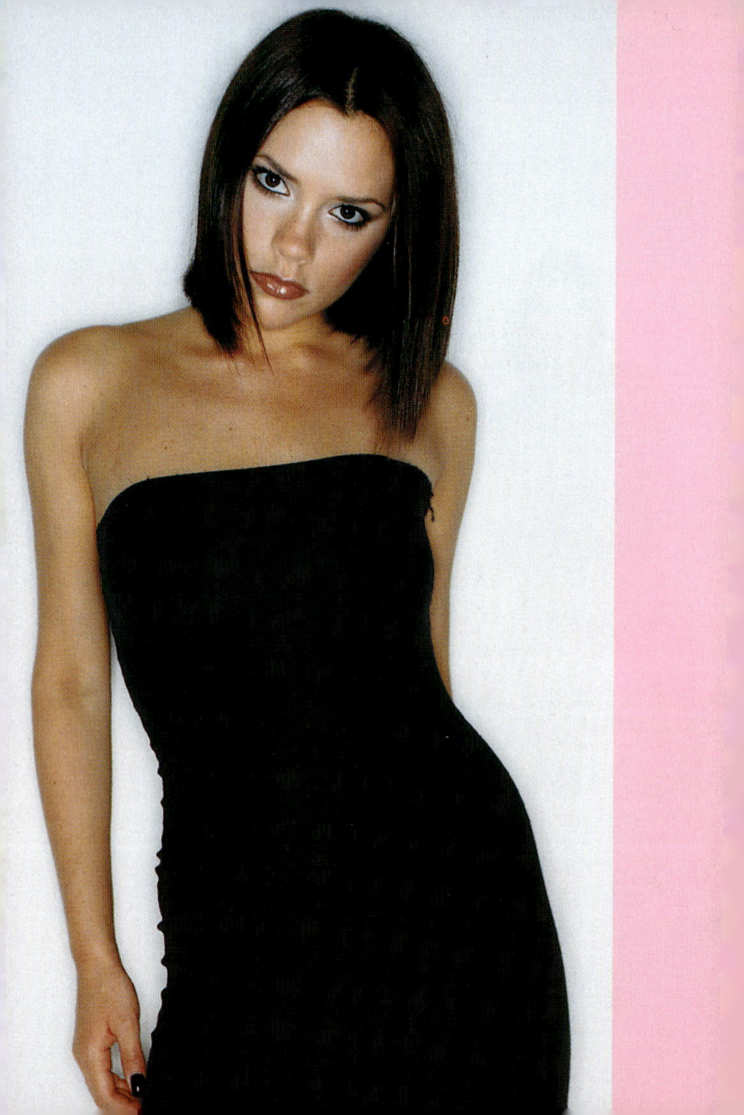

"I like being smart. I may wear tracksuit bottoms or jeans around the house, but I very rarely go out like that."

"I'm a worrier, a bag of nervous energy."

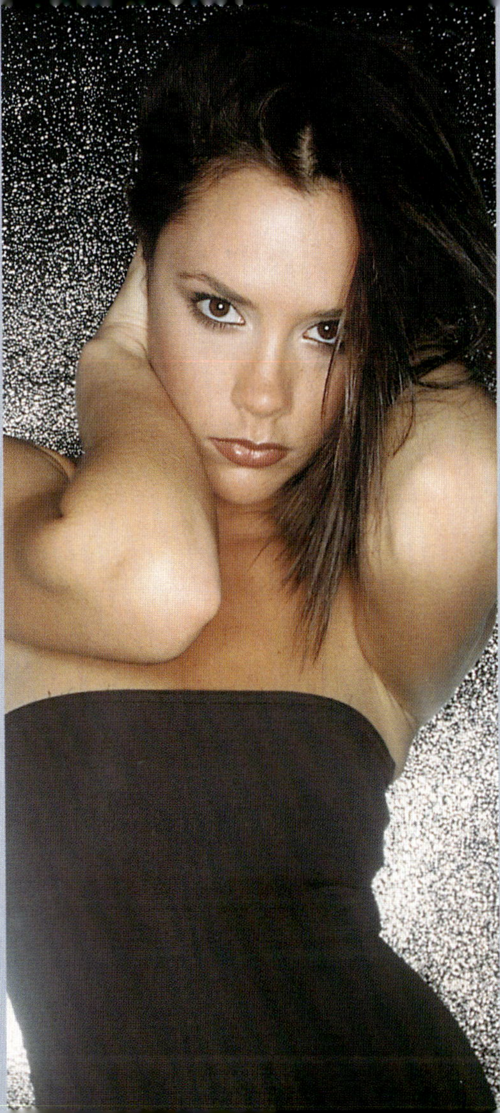

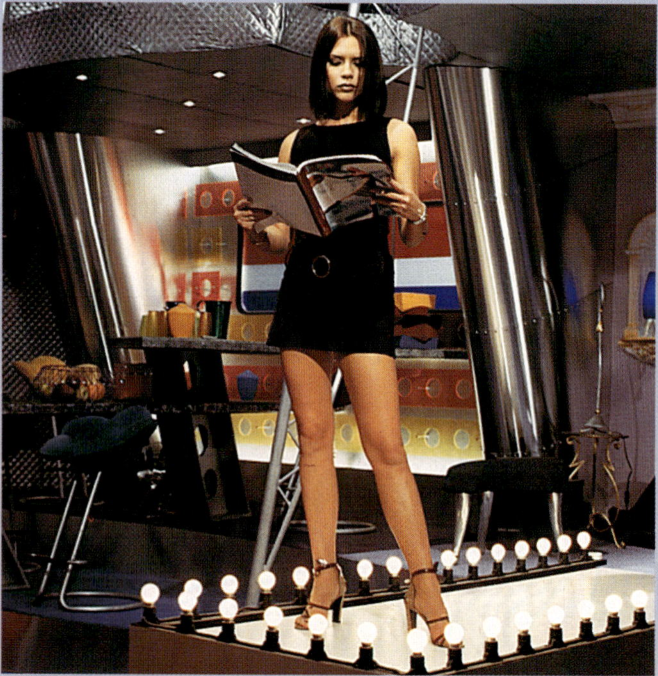

"I used to appear on stage when I was very young - two or three. When I was about eight I did a show where I was dressed up in a bright yellow top hat and tails with sequins all over it, yellow fishnet tights and yellow tap shoes with yellow bows. I tap danced to *If My Friends Could See Me Now*, that Shirley MacLaine song from *Sweet Charity* – and I **was** Shirley MacLaine."

"Act like a lady and you'll be treated like one."

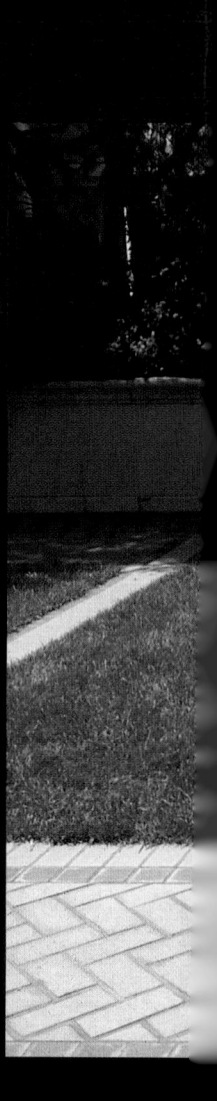

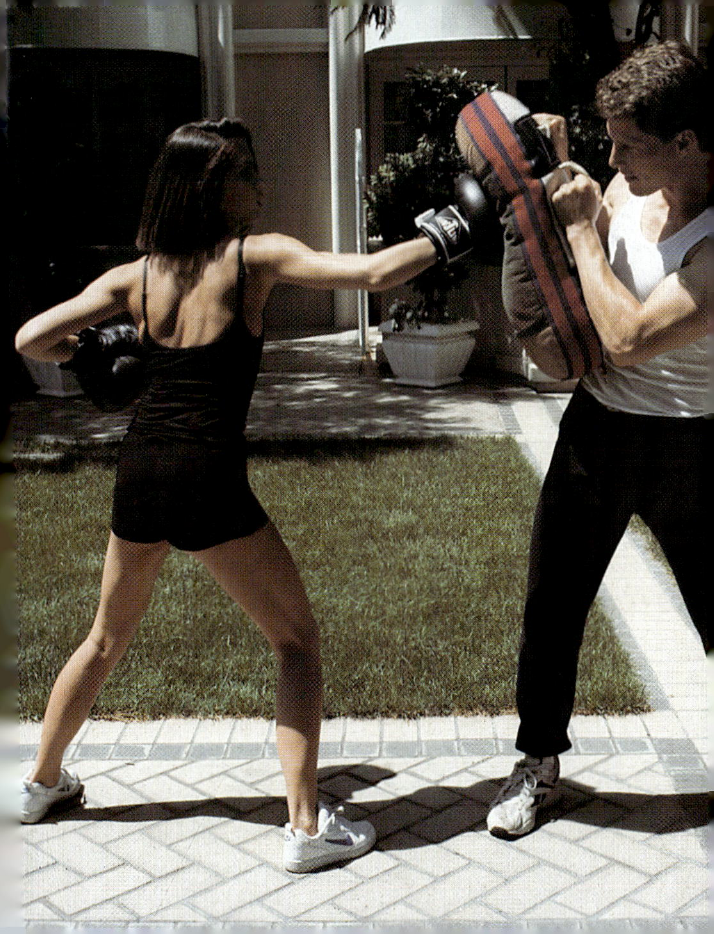

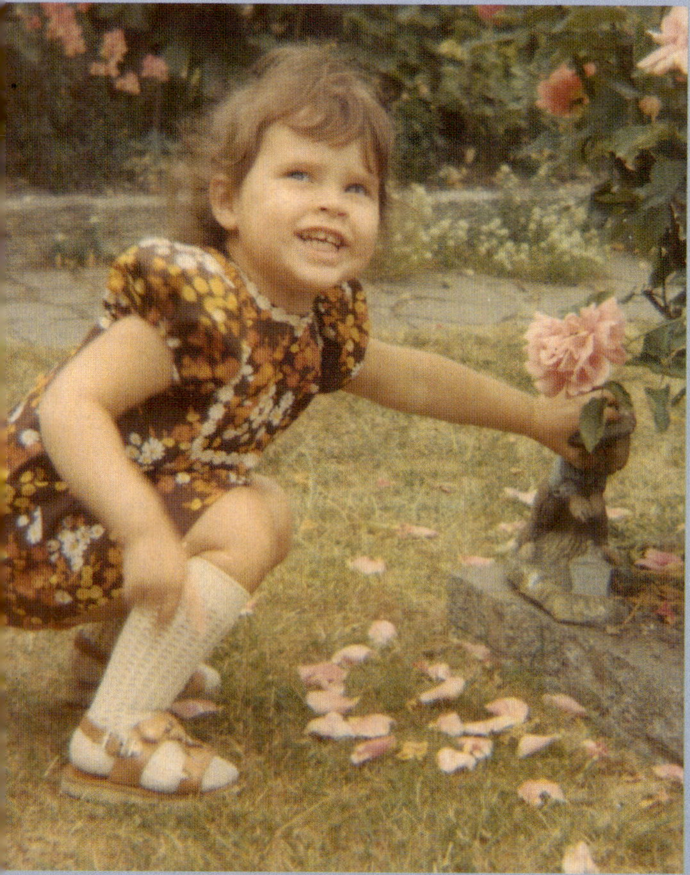

"I'm supposedly the posh one, but I don't consider myself posh. I do like designer clothes, I suppose, and at least my mum was happy when she found out that was my nickname."

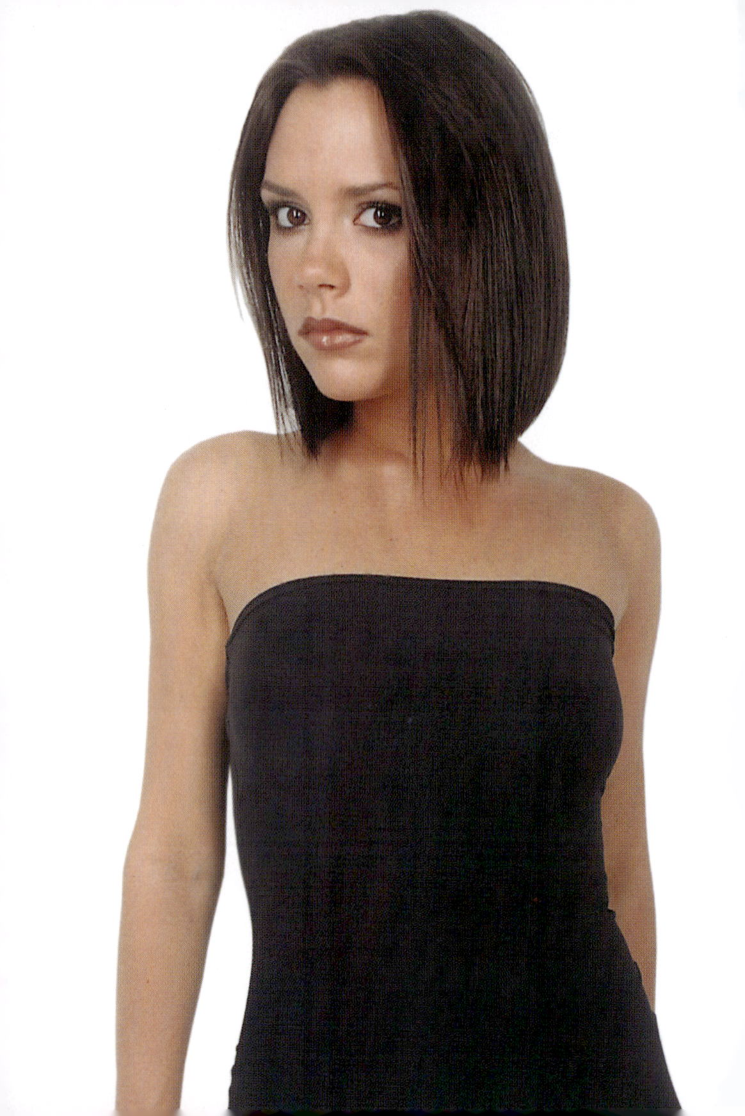

"It doesn't matter what you do as long as you do it like a lady."

"I'd like to put *smiles* on as many people's faces as I can with our music."

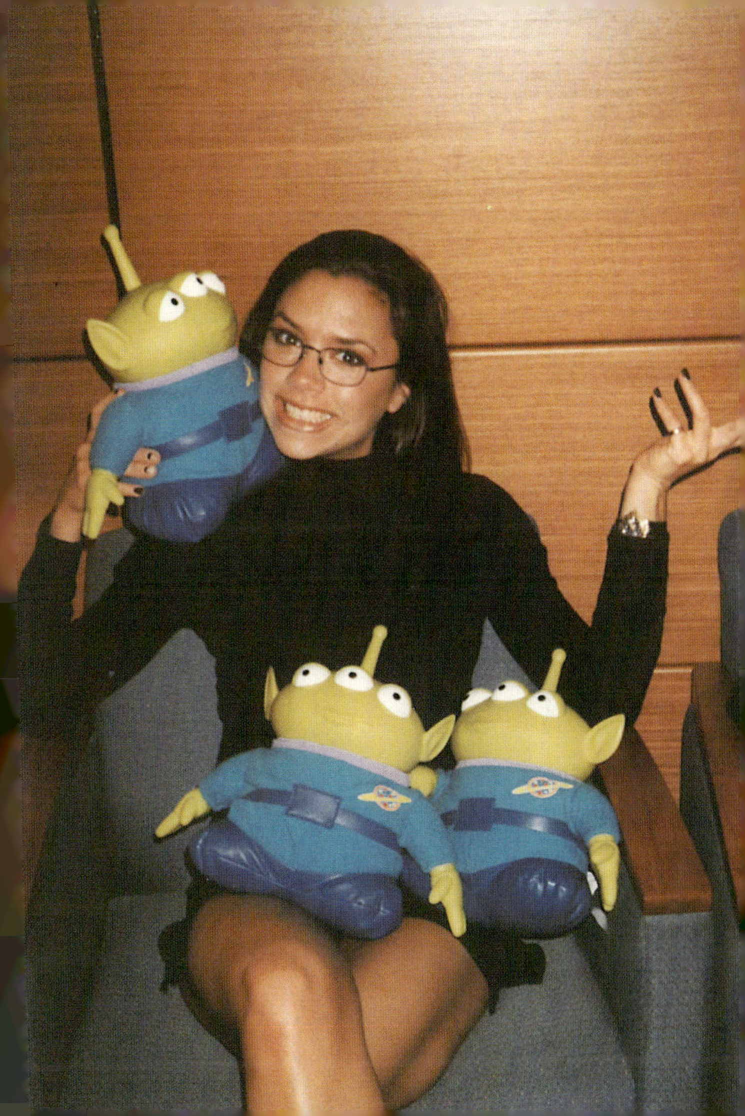

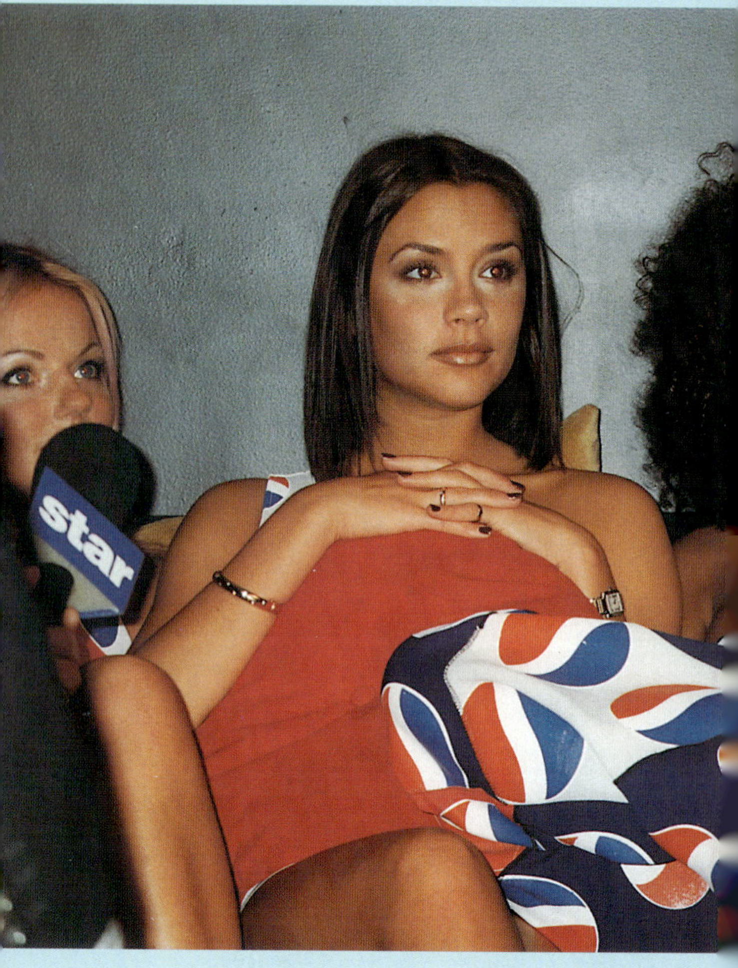
star

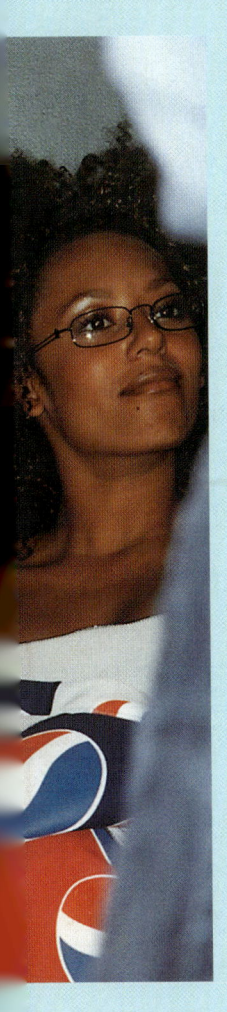

"Nowadays I'm amazed that I have photographers chasing me about. I came out of my house the other day and got in my car. There were all these people with long lenses hanging about and pointing their cameras and I thought to myself, 'What are they taking pictures of trees for?' Then I realised it was me they were shooting."

"I really like basic foods. I eat a lot of toast and vegetables and fruit – dried fruit as well. Mostly I eat steamed or boiled vegetables with a bit of fish or chicken – I'm quite a boring eater, really."

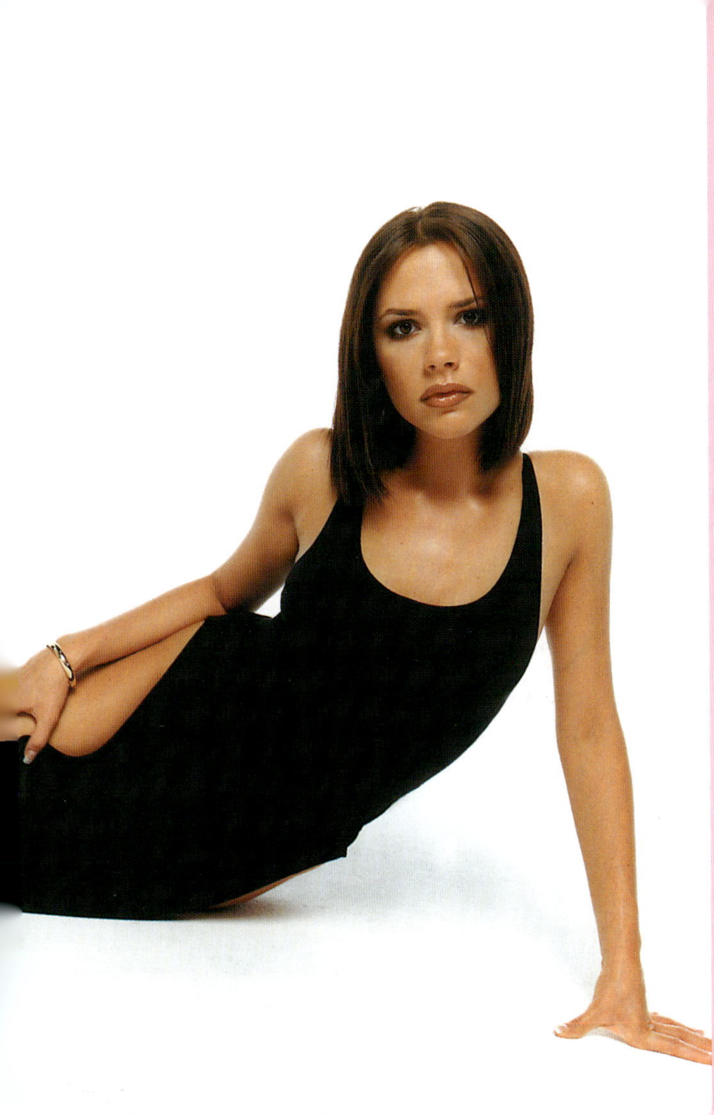

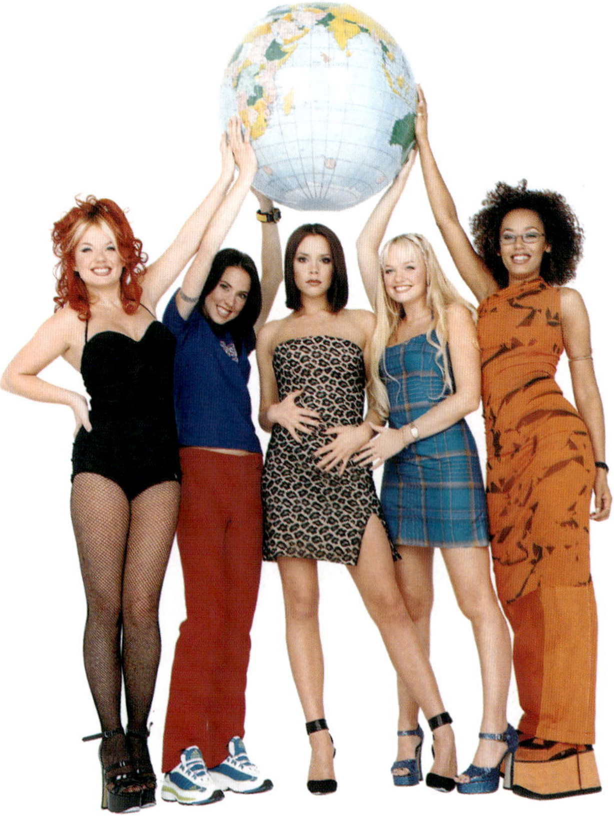

"We want to be a household name. We want to be a fairy Liquid or Ajax."

"When I was really young, everyone at school used to look at models in magazines and we all thought that we had to look like them. Well, you haven't got to be that way. It doesn't matter if you're a size 8 or 88, short, tall, long-haired, or short-haired. As long as you accept yourself and make the best of yourself, you're going to make yourself happier."

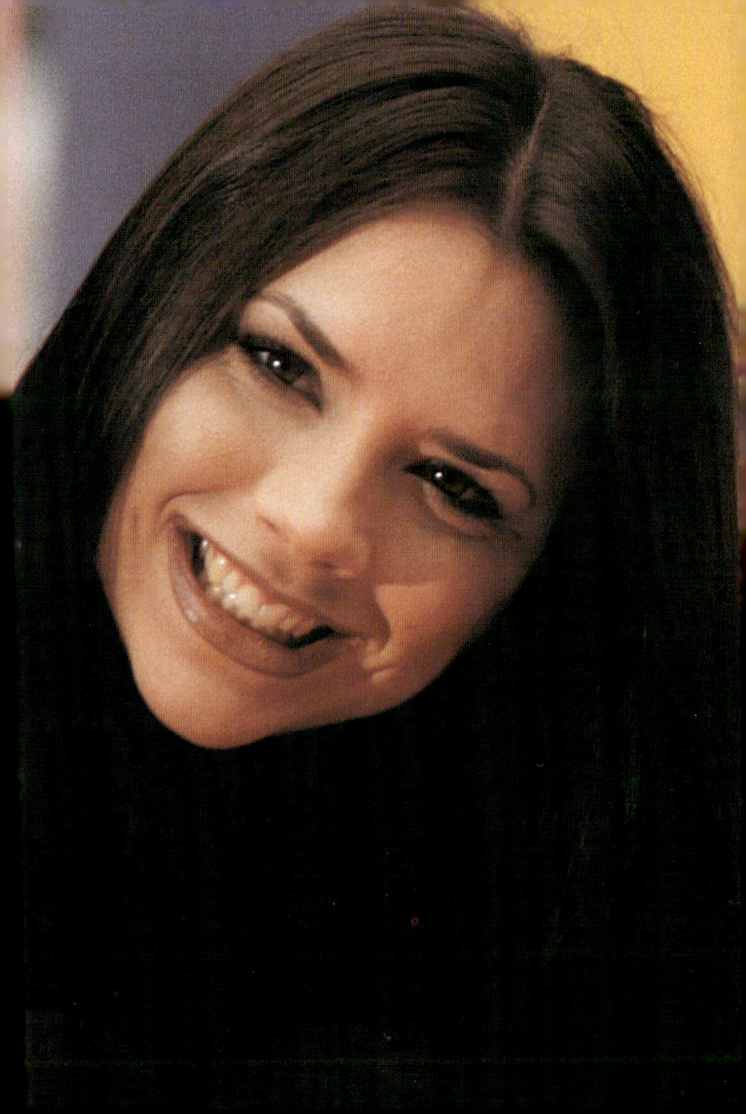

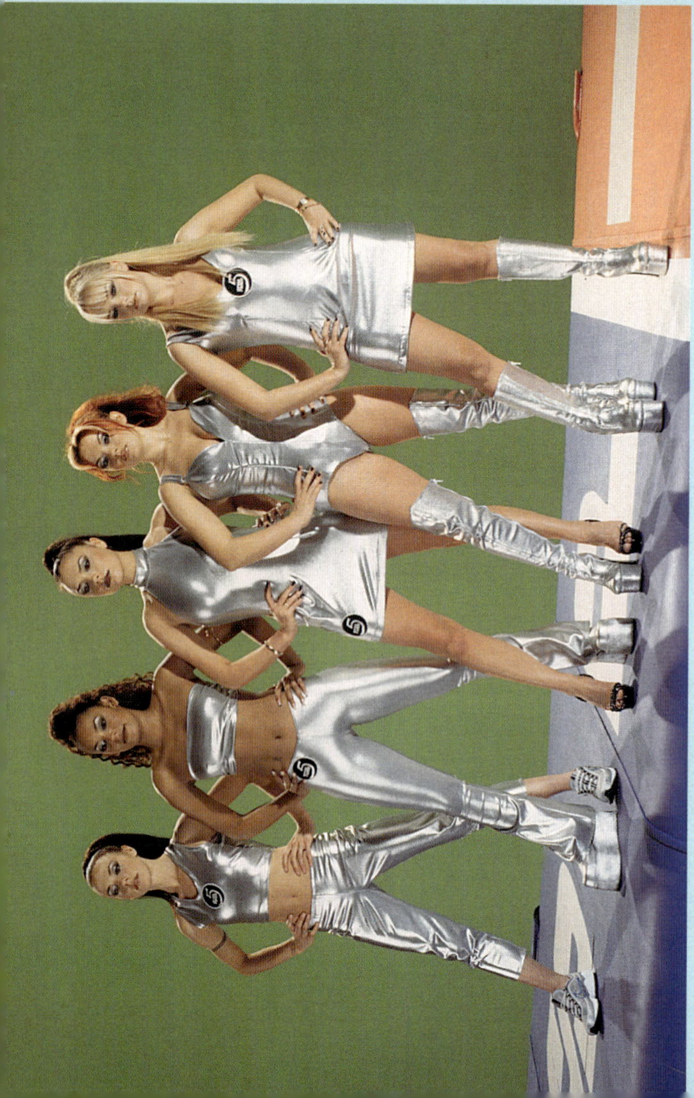

"When I was little I always thought I wanted to be **famous**. But you could never dream up what's happened to us. It's a bit **out of the ordinary**."

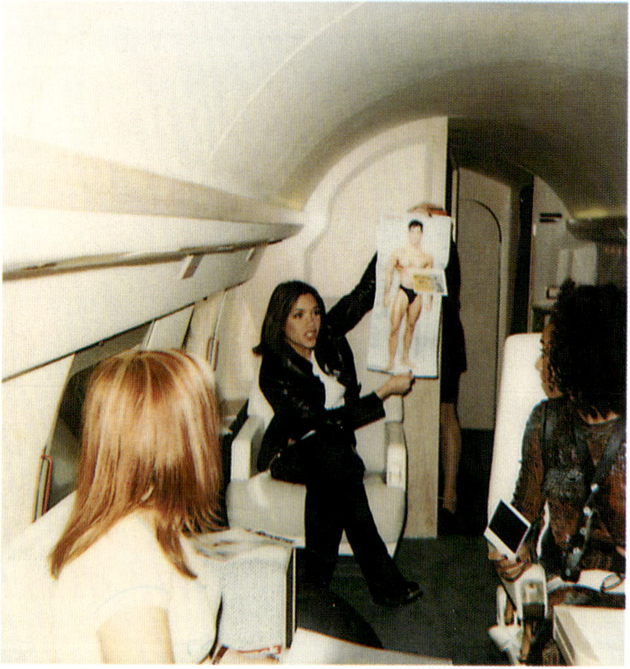

"The best things about a man are that he should be a **friend**, have a sense of **humour**, a good pair of **shoes** and a sixpack."

"I love what I do, even if some people think I look miserable in photos because I don't smile much. That's not miserable, that's just me – I don't like my dimples!"

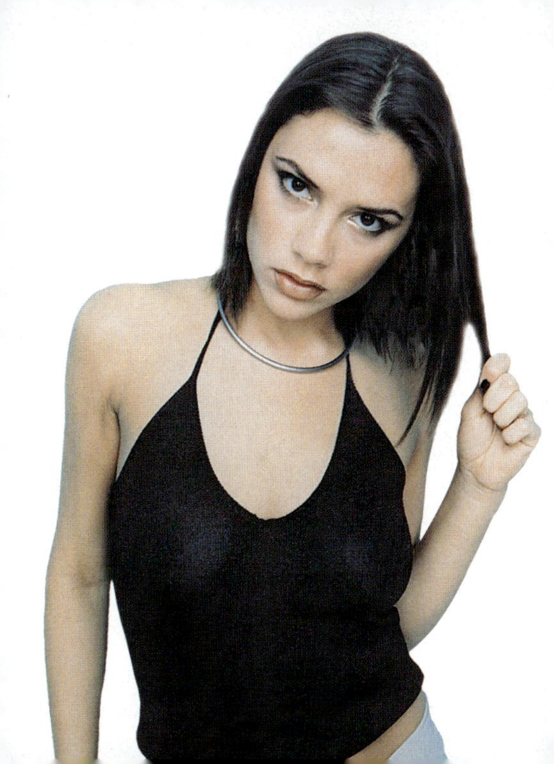

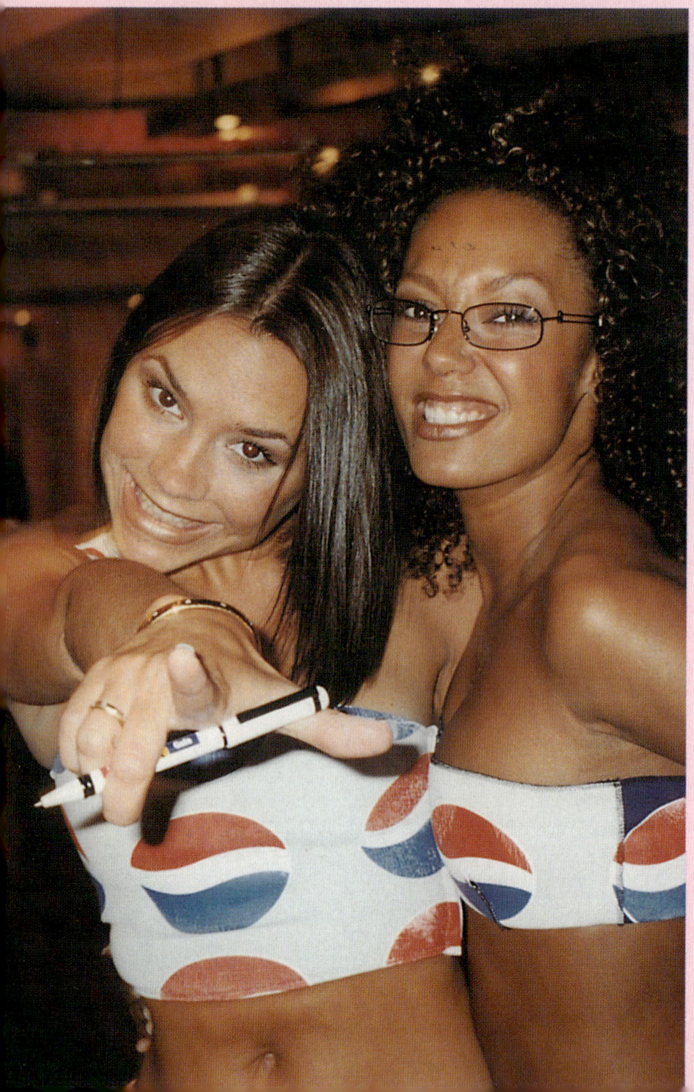

"Even though I was brought up to be a strong woman, sometimes it's not until you meet other people who think the same as you that it really all falls into place."

"It's a **great** feeling to get up on stage and perform after spending such a lot of time writing the music."

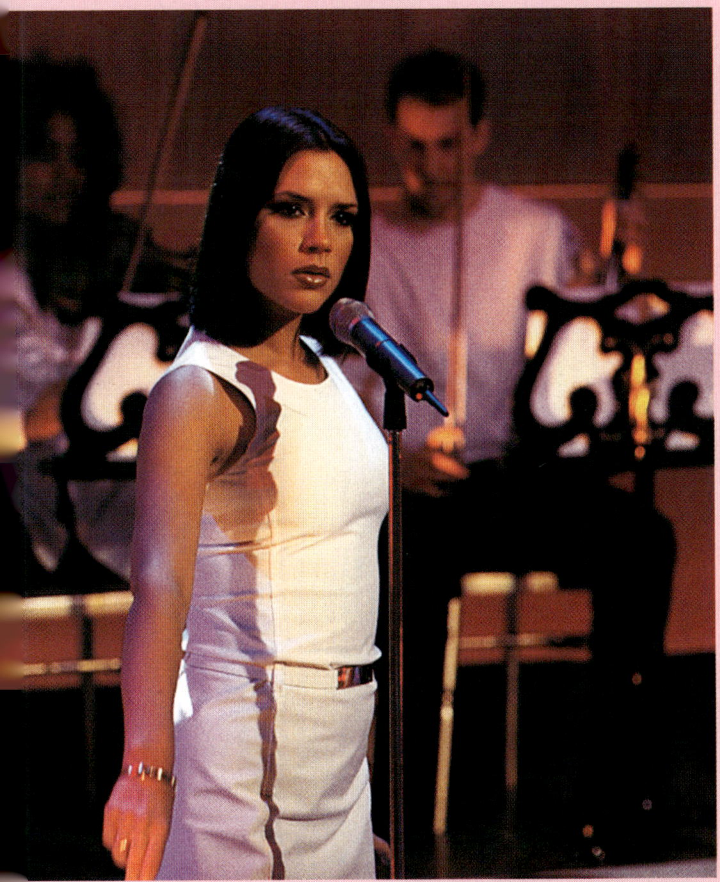

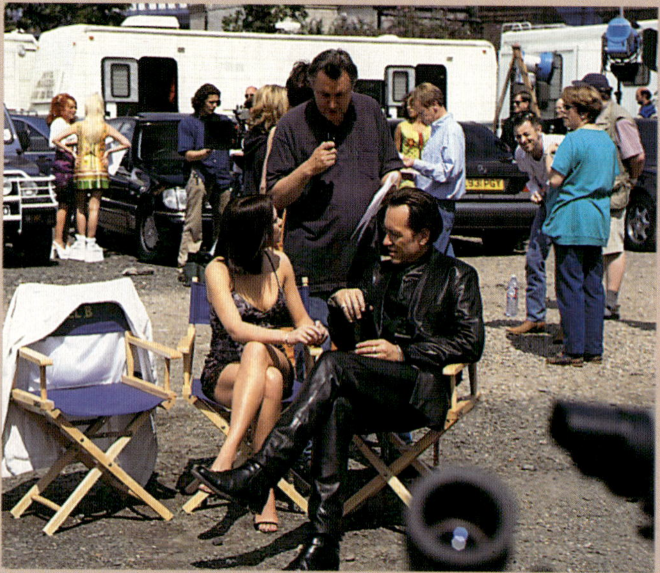

"You get a lot more respect if you've got a bit of a brain. If not, then just pretend to have one!"

"I really enjoy my life now."

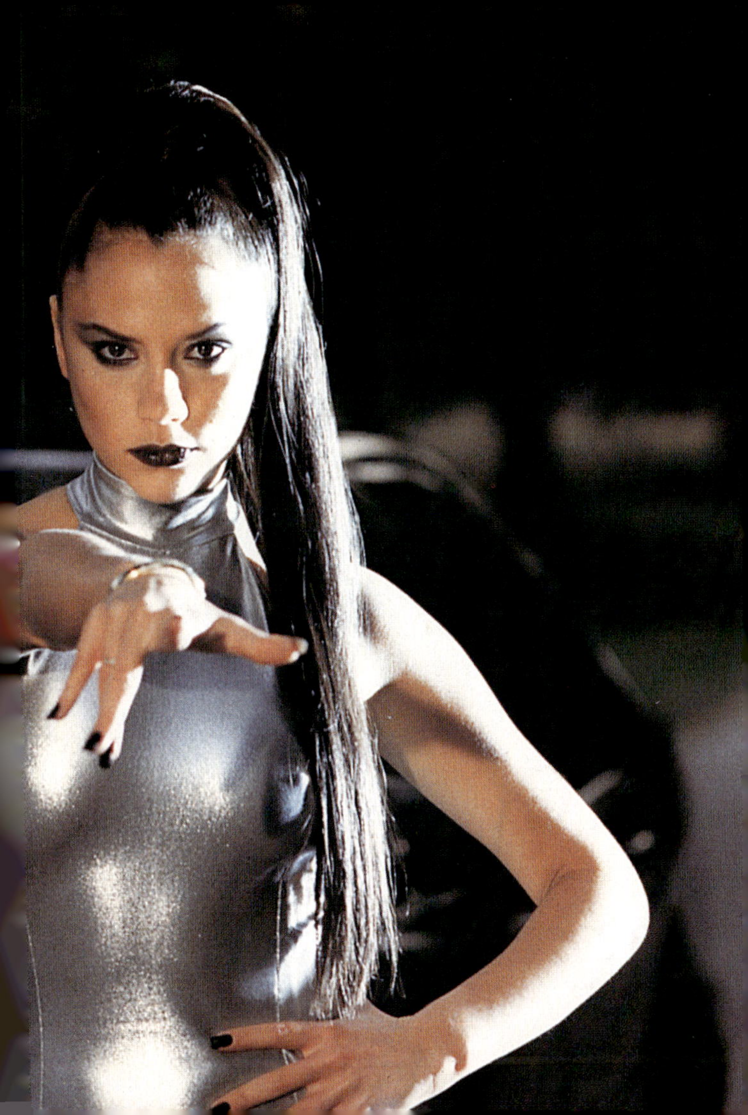

"This is me with my sister Louise – my best friend."

Louise

"I like spending a lot of time with my family and friends, going shopping and eating a lot of toast, but I really hate two-faced people and sushi."

looking happy at the end of our Taiwan trip!

"I think you have to be strong in yourself to treat people the same whoever they are, rather than be impressed and won over by how much money or fame somebody's got."

THANKS FOR READING MY BOOK!

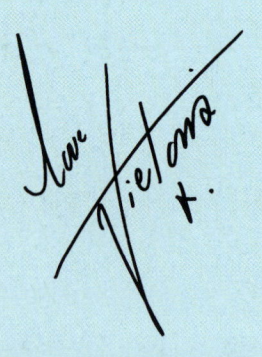

love Victoria x.

GET THE SET! FOUR MORE OFFICIAL MINIBOOKS TO COLLECT

SPICE GIRLS OFFICIAL PUBLICATIONS